Contents

Ordnance Survey maps that cover this area

1:50,000 Landranger

132 - North West Norfolk
143 - Ely & Wisbech

1:25,000 Explorer

23 (250) - Norfolk Coast (West)
24 (251) - Norfolk Coast (Central)
236 - King's Lynn, Downham Market, Swaffham
238 - East Dereham & Aylsham

For details of public transport - call 08456 020 121 or 0870 608 2 608

THE COUNTRY CODE

* Use gates and stiles to cross fences, hedges and walls
* Guard against all risks of fire
* Take special care on country roads
* Help to keep water clean
* Fasten all gates
* Keep to public paths across farmland
* Leave livestock, crops and machinery alone
* Enjoy the countryside and respect its life and work
* Protect wildlife, plants and trees
* Keep dogs under control
* Make no unnecessary noise
* Take all your litter home

1 - Stiffkey & The Coast Path

Distance: 4.5 mls - 7.2 km (about 2 hours)

O.S. Landranger 132/Explorer 24 (251)
Grid reference 974430

Everyone knows England's greatest Admiral was "a good ol' Norfolk boy" from Burnham Thorpe. What many don't know is that this same stretch of North Norfolk coast gave us three other great seamen.

The first, born at nearby Salthouse, was Sir Christopher Myngs - who had entered service as a cabin-boy, unlike many seventeenth century 'gentleman' officers of Charles II's navy. In turn, his cabin-boy was Sir John Narborough, from Cockthorpe; and the cabin-boy of Sir John Narborough was Sir Cloudesley Shovel also from Cockthorpe. All three from the same neighbourhood and humble parentage and all destined to become Admirals and receive knighthoods.

Stiffkey once had a quay and a harbour, but is now separated from the sea by some 600 acres of salt marsh. It is famed for its cockles called 'Stewkey Blues', and for being the home of of its colourful and tragic rector of the 1920s and 1930s, the Revd. Harold Davidson.

1. - Start from the parking area by the small green, with the village sign, near the church of St. John, the Baptist. The churchyard once boasted a second church, St. Mary's, long since gone, and nearby stands Bacon's early 17th. century hall. Turn west along Church Street. Although now subject to a 20 mph speed limit this is the main coast road so take great care as you follow this narrow winding road past flint and brick cottages to a junction. Turn left into Bridge Street, toward Cockthorpe, and cross the Stiffkey. This river, one of only a few that seek the sea along the north Norfolk coast, rises twenty miles away near Melton Constable. Out of Stiffkey take the left fork (Langham & Binham) toward Cockthorpe and follow this narrow country 'holloway' uphill. Pass the modest church of All Saints, Cockthorpe, opposite a farm, and maintained by the Norfolk Churches Trust. After a further 200 yards turn left along a signposted track by a phone-box and farm.

2. - This gravel track soon gives way to a pleasant, hedged lane as it winds northwards. This leads to a fieldgate that opens out onto Cockthorpe Common. Continue along this grassy pasture with a low hill forming on your right and where the field narrows pass a small wood on your left.

Where the field and hill swing away to the right and by the corner of the wood cross a good, strong footbridge over the stream. Follow the track to a second footbridge spanning the clear waters of the Stiffkey and follow the clear path through the trees toward the coast road.

A far cry from the early days of Norfolk Ramblers when early members of the first groups (Norwich and Lynn), led by that most redoubtable and indefatigable of true Norfolk pioneering ramblers Reg Money of Dereham, followed a near impenetrable route that crossed these streams with precarious old logs and fallen trees!

Just before the main coast road turn right along a good, permissive path that leads, parallel with the road, to the Stiffkey bridge. This welcome linking path has been provided by Stiffkey Farms as a safe alternative to the roadside verge. Thank you!

3. - At the bridge cross the road (with care) and follow the signposted riverside path to the main coast seabank. Climb the bank and turn left along the Coast Path. Follow this marshside path for about ¾ mile along the National Trust's Stiffkey Salt Marshes to an open parking area by a large wood.

4. - Turn left and follow the stony track due south into Stiffkey. At the main road, cross to the footpath and turn right back to the green.

2 - Burnham Thorpe

Distance: 4.5 mls - 7.2 km (about 2 hours)

O.S. Landranger 132/Explorer 24 (251)
Grid reference 852418

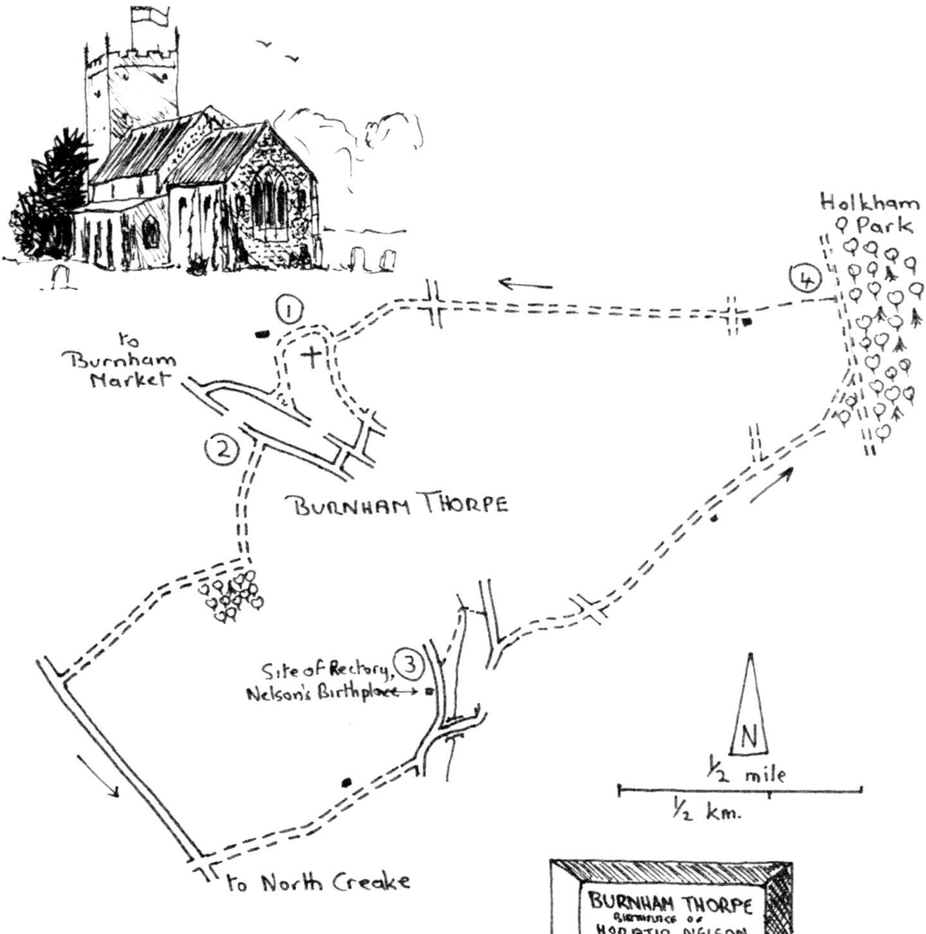

Burnham Thorpe's greatest claim to fame must surely be its 200 year link with that greatest of English sea faring heroes and Norfolk's most famous son - Admiral Lord Horatio Nelson. For it was in the old rectory, alas long since gone, that Horatio was born on September 29th 1758.

The village has probably altered little since and still possesses much rural charm. We share some of the sights, sounds and smells that the young Horatio must have known as he too explored the local paths and lanes.

The modest flint church of All Saints holds many Nelson 'relics', and it is here that his father - rector for 46 years - lies buried. His son was destined for more lofty surroundings for he rests beneath the dome of St. Paul's.

18 months before his death he wrote "Most probably I shall never see dear, dear Burnham again, but I have the satisfaction in thinking that my bones will probably lie with my father's in the village that gave me birth".

1. - Start from the grassy car-park area on the north side of the church and follow the track round, past the east end, and walk south towards the village, past the playing field. At the crossroads opposite The Pightle (an enclosure or pound), turn right to the Walsingham Road junction, with the fine village sign, presented by the Royal Navy, on your left. Cross into Blacksmith's Lane, then turn right into Creake Road. Follow to just past the small crescent of houses on your left.

2. - Turn left along the track, with a left hedge, uphill. Turn right at the top and follow past the wood.

From along here are wide views of the surrounding countryside to the coast. The view stretches from Burnham Norton church (originally there were seven Burnhams), with Scolt Head Island beyond, past Burnham Overy mill, and east to the pines of Holkham beach. Further inland may be seen the obelisk in Holkham Park.

Passing the wood continue downhill to the road. Cross and turn left (facing the traffic) and carefully follow for nearly $^1/_2$ mile to where a sandy track crosses. Turn left and follow this green lane past a fine, large barn to a road. Bear left and follow to a junction and bridge over the River Burn; but keep left along the road passing the flint garden wall of the old rectory with its commemorative plaque and inscription.

3. - A few yards further on a stile on your right gives access to a path alongside the stream. The Burn rises south of South Creake and runs to the sea at Burnham Overy, and Is one of the few rivers that run to the north coast of Norfolk. At the footbridge turn right and cross to follow the left field-edge path to the road. Turn right to the bend where a track goes off to the left. Turn along this and follow to another road. Cross and follow the sandy track uphill and past the remains of an old barn. The track crests the hill and continues ahead, past a left junction, toward the great park of Holkham. Shortly before the park-wall the track bears left, alongside a small triangle of trees, to the park-wall, and you pick up with the grassy track running alongside. This is the line of a Roman road that ran several miles inland from the coast.

Following the wall and, about 100 yards past an iron-gate, turn left at the first field boundary.

4. - Follow this field-edge path running to the left of the hedge, This leads past a solidly built, traditional brick and pantile barn. Passing this cross the junction and continue ahead along the track, After crossing a narrow lane the church tower comes into view and the path drops gently back down to it.

3 - Coxford & Broomsthorpe

Distance: 5.5 mls - 8.9 km (about 2.5 hours)

O.S. Landranger 132/Explorer 238
Grid reference 849295

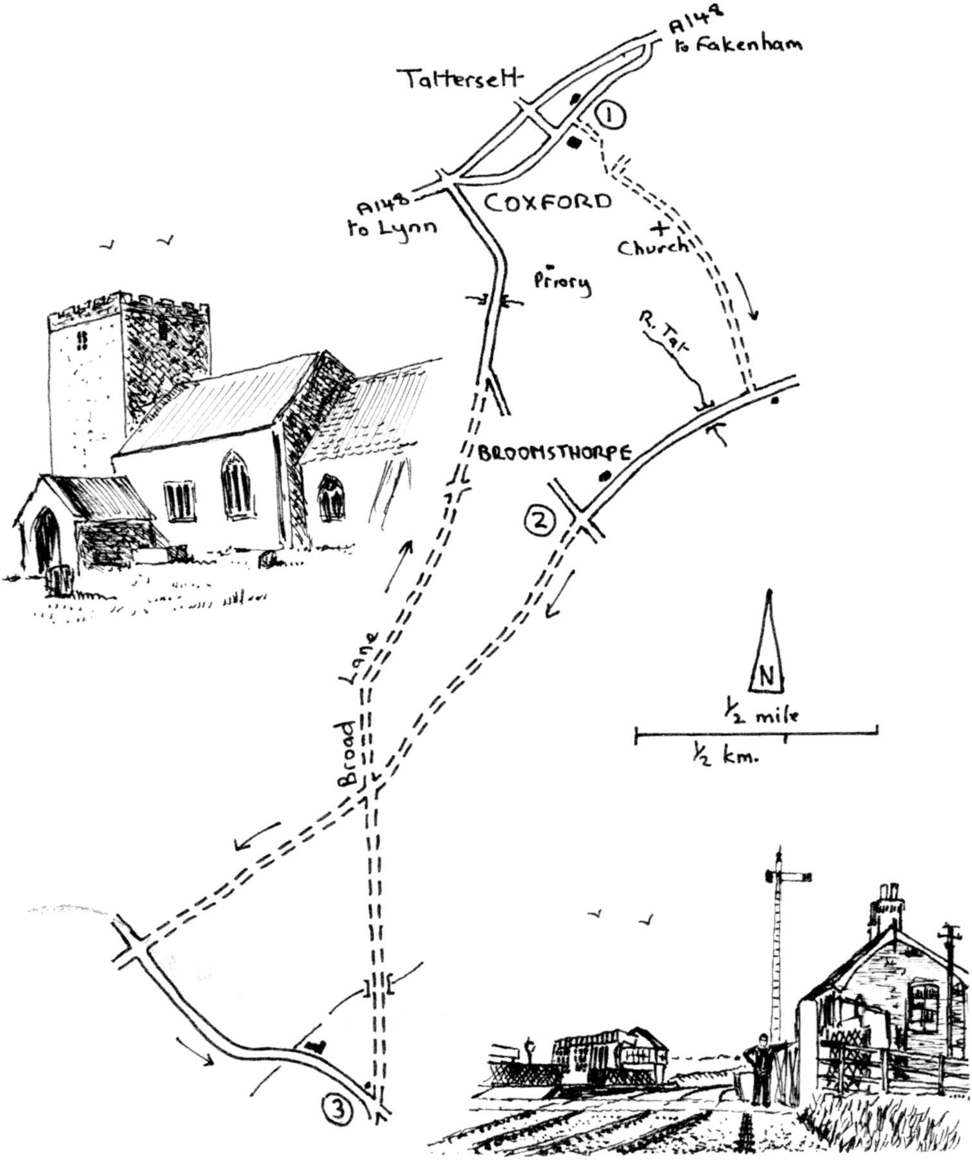

Coxford, once Cokesford, is a small, quiet hamlet, situated just off the main A148, on the Fakenham side of East Rudham.
Indeed, it lies on the very edge of that parish, just on the boundary between West and North Norfolk.

Along this edge, and running roughly northwest to southeast is the River Tat, which rises by Syderstone Common and joins the Wensum after just four miles, just through Tatterford.

This is supreme Norfolk countryside at its best, and well off the beaten track.

1. - Start from the eastern end of Coxford, just past Manor Farm, to follow a short, signposted lane past the Reception building to a kissing-gate by the Manor Park caravan park. Cross the grassy field to the stile and gate in the right corner and cross the pasture, aiming just to the right of the church, to a second kissing-gate near the corner. Now pick up with the track that heads past the church; a plain and simple building with traces of ancient wall-painting, and an old memorial inscription on the chancel floor.

The gently rising ground gives good views across the wooded Tat valley. Continue along the track to join a country road and turn right.

This pleasant lane, with its views of Manor Farm, the church, and fragments of Coxford Priory, leads past woods and over the crystal-clear waters of the Tat, to Broomsthorpe and back into West Norfolk.

2. - At the next road junction cross into the track opposite, an ancient lane. At the grassy 'crossroads' cross over Broad Lane into another track that rises gently over a low rise, with Rudham in the far distance, down to a road.

Turn left and follow the road past the extensive buildings that mark the former East Rudham railway station.

About one-and-a-half miles south of the village this once busy station had important and extensive sidings handling grain and and farm produce for the Midland and Great Northern Railway (M&GN).

This alien line - for this was Great Eastern territory - not only brought holidaymakers from Birmingham and the Midlands to Cromer, Yarmouth and Norwich, but also served a score of small rural Norfolk settlements right across the county. The last railway to come to Norfolk was also the first to go, in 1959.

Beyond the station continue to the next road junction.

3. - From here may be seen the buildings and tower of former RAF West Raynham. Just past the bungalow turn left along a grassy track which soon crosses over the mellow old rail-bridge. Keep walking north along Broad Lane, crossing over your outward route, along a more winding section rich in wild flowers. Cross a road and continue along a now narrower, lush, and very old lane to a road. Bear left along this past rushing water, rough meadows, and the ruins of the Priory back into Coxford.

St. Mary's Augustinian Priory, rebuilt on this site early in Henry III's reign, was acquired after Dissolution by the Townshend family who proceeded to use its stone to build a new house in 1619.

The first stone removed broke a man's leg. The church steeple fell on a house nearby, killing a man inside; others having to save themselves in 'Fright and Flight'.

The new buildings were continually being 'reft in sunder' so were abandoned in 1621 for a new site, new foundations, and new materials

At the crossroads, just before the main A148, turn right through the hamlet and back over the clear waters of the Tat to the start.

4 - The Woottons

Distance: 5.5 mls - 8.9 km (about 2.5 hours)

O.S. Landranger 132/Explorer 23 (250)
Grid reference 640228

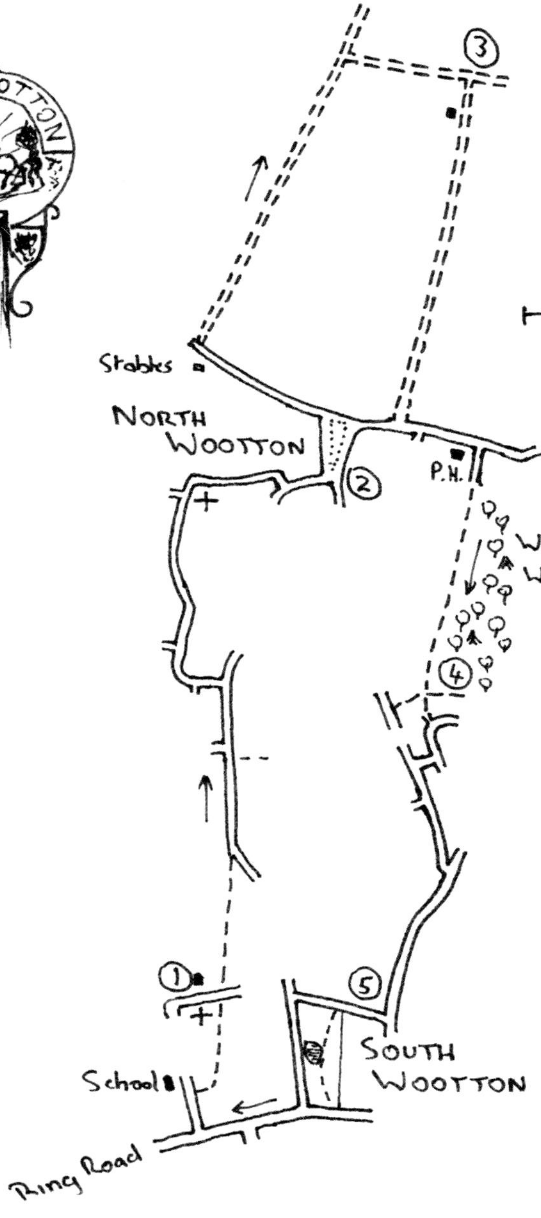

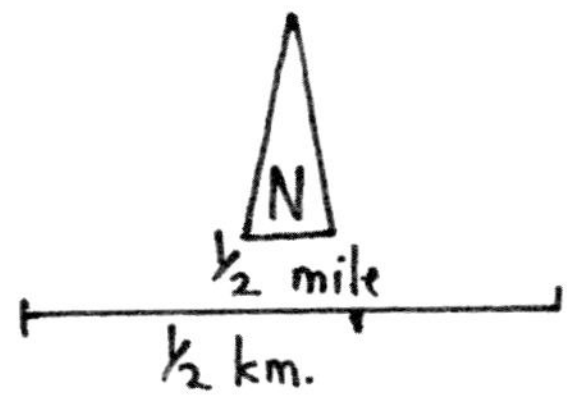

On the doorstep of Lynn, here is an urban, or rather suburban ramble around the Woottons. Although dominated by ever-growing modern commuter estates, there are still pleasant corners and glimpses of older, more tradItional buildings and charm.

1. - Start from the car-park by South Wootton Village Hall, opposite St Mary's church, and turn left out of the car-park, past a bungalow, and then left through an iron kissing-gate along a fenced, grassy path. Continue over several stiles until you join a road (Nursery Lane). Follow this road up over the hill and past Spinney Close. Shortly after, where all Saints' Drive begins, Nursery Lane turns left past older houses, a shop and garage, and continues to a small cluster of older cottages and houses by All Saints church, North Wootton. Past the junction with Station Road, Nursery Lane turns sharp right into Manor Road. Follow this past a pleasant mix of buildings and a small, modern green, complete with a young oak with surrounding seat and a recently erected war memorial. Pass this junction with All Saints' Drive and continue along Manor Road to Priory Lane and the village green.

2. - Bear left along the green past the older heart of the village to Gatehouse Lane. Here turn left, past the Rugby Club, and continue to just beyond Greenacres Riding School.

Turn right, through a gate, onto an area of conservation walks and permissive paths, and follow the line of this old railway line (Lynn to Hunstanton). This section is quite wide as the railway was double-tracked from Lynn to the Royal Station at Wolferton, but only single-tracked beyond!

Follow the path toward the Babingley River, for a little over $^{1}/_{2}$ mile (just past a former concrete platelayers' hut) and, over a small bridge by a pumping station, you turn right along an open track.

Follow this for about $^{1}/_{4}$ mile to two sets of double-gates opposite each other.

3. - Turn right along the hedged track past the farm buildings. This rather pleasant lane eventually brings you onto Ling Common Road, back in North Wootton. Turn left and, just past the House on the Green, turn right into Little Carr Road. Follow this past houses, and keep ahead as it narrows into a path that runs south just inside Wootton Woods. This path leads over two simple footbridges close to the houses, then along a more open section before coming to a T-junction at the Leylandii hedged gardens of another estate (The Birches).

4. - A path crosses left to right. Turn right and immediately left along a hedged path into the estate. Turn left and right to follow the estate road through The Birches. At the next junction turn right, out onto Priory Lane. Turn left here, past St. Augustine's Way. Continue to the junction with Castle Rising Road and turn right to follow this road uphill with its older 'ribbon development' houses. Follow for about 600 yards to the junction with Common Lane and turn right to South Wootton green.

5. - At the green turn left past the large pond (once one of three in the village) and its attendant flocks of duck and geese, to the metal kissing-gate and stile onto Low Road.

Turn right and follow this rather noisy section past the end of Nursery Lane toward Edward Benefer Way (northern ring road).

At Hall Lane turn right and follow past The Boltons before turning right along a signposted tarmac footpath (part of the Sandringham Cycleway) that leads back to St. Mary's church.

5 - Great Ouse & River Nar

Distance: 6 mls - 9.7 km (about 2.5 hours)

O.S. Landranger 132/Explorer 23 (250)
Grid reference 618196

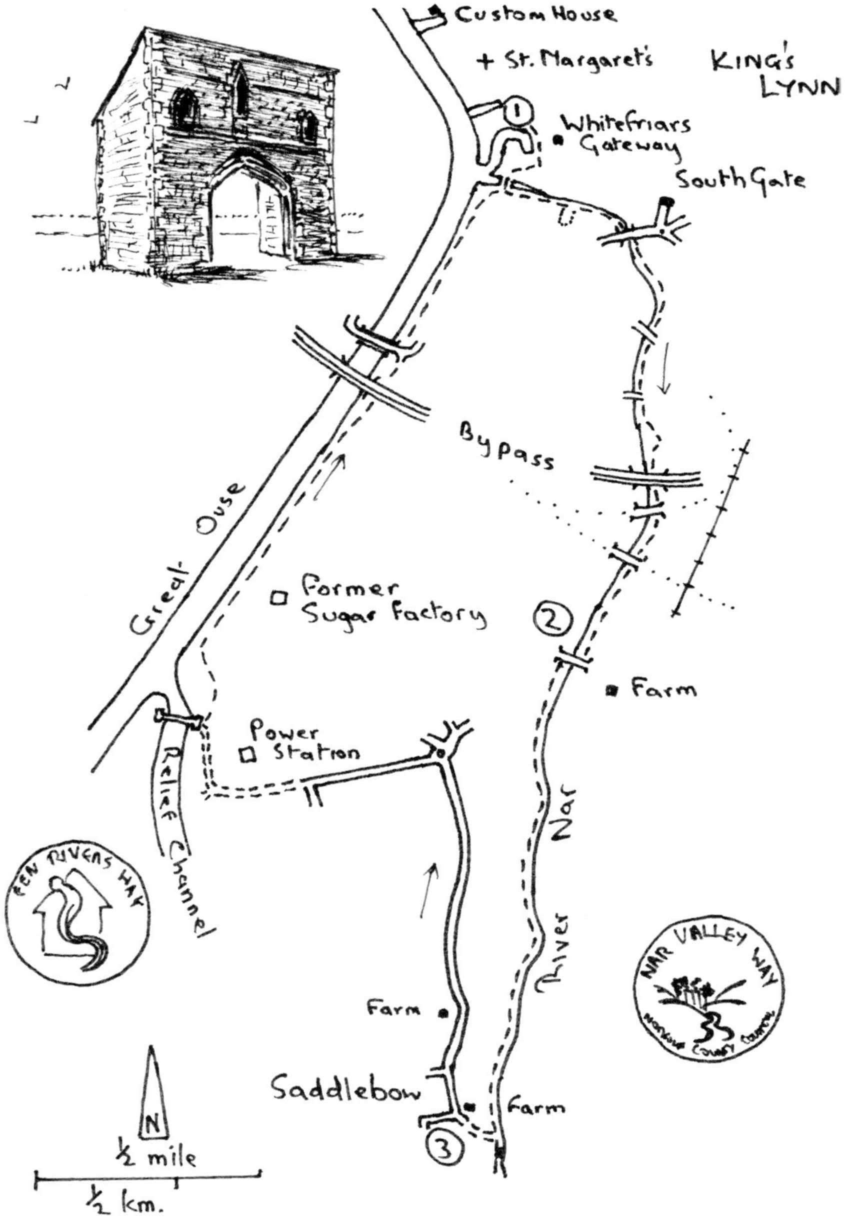

Rivers, in particular the Great Ouse and the Nar, have provided the life blood of Lynn over many centuries, and have shaped its boundaries and its fortunes. Both rivers have lost much industry In recent years but their former towpaths now provide perfect routes for long-distance paths.

The 32 mile Nar Valley Way runs from the heart of Norfolk, near Dereham, and follows the valley and river to the Great Ouse. The 50 mile Fen Rivers Way follows the Great Ouse from Cambridge to Lynn, and the Iceni Way is an 80 mile route from Peddars Way, that follows the Little and Great Ouse rivers to Lynn, then the Wash coast to Hunstanton and the Norfolk Coast Path.

1. - Start from the large, Long Term, gravel car-park off Boal Street, near the end of the Millfleet. This area was the site of Paul's Mill and also the North Sea Steamship Co. As you leave the car- park, bear left around the outside, following the concrete floodwall. This leads past the Boal Quay with fishing boats, and past the now silted-up former mouth of the River Nar.

Follow the track between the wall and river as it climbs up onto a bank. Note the small mediaeval gateway of the former Carmelites, or Whitefriars. The bank crosses the Nar and immediately over the outfall (1987) turn sharp left, down and along the riverside - Friars Fleet. This path runs opposite the now derelict boatyards that fringed this part of The Friars.

The large reed-filled, concrete-walled creek on your right is Blubber Creek. Lynn's important whaling industry was considered no ungainful concern and boasted a sizeable fleet which brought the cut-up mammals back to the two Narside blubber-houses. The Greenland Fishery still stands near Boal Street. This area must have had quite a pungent atmosphere when the huge coppers were operating.

Follow the river past the South-Gates and, at the roadbridge, cross the road and the bridge to take the path along the left of the river. This leads past the former gasworks to follow the river southwards. Pass a bridge still with its railway. This spur ran from the main line, across the Nar and Millfleet, to serve the Boal Quay and the entire South Quay to the Purfleet. The path passes another bridge and sluice. Near here stood the famous muck-works (West Norfolk Fertilisers). Keeping as close to the river as possible you pass under the southern bypass, and soon after you pass over the old M&GN line that linked South Lynn station with the Great Eastern Railway, then the main M&GN line. This ran from the Midlands and North via Sutton Bridge and South Lynn station (which stood here between the rivers) before crossing Norfolk via Melton Constable to Cromer, Norwich and Yarmouth. It closed In 1959.

After passing a large grain store, on the far side of the river, you come to another bridge near farm buildings.

2. - Cross over and continue along the western path. Initially open, after a stile it becomes hedged, and quite lush. After just over 1/2 mile, and about 150 yards before a banktop house, turn right down a track and past a farm to the road.

3. - At the road bear right and follow northwards, past a junction to a roundabout near the power-station. Turn left along the road and on the first sharp left corner keep ahead along a track. This bears right over a stile, and is the access road to the Cut-Off Channel Tail Sluice. Pass through a kissing-gate and just before the sluice, turn right through another. Follow the riverside path under the bypass bridge again to the next bridge (Cut Bridge). Cross the road and follow the riverside path, with magnificent views of Lynn's skyline, back to the mouth of the Nar and your starting point.

6 - Wiggenhall St. Mary Magdalen

Distance: 6 mls - 9.7 km (about 2.5 hours)

O.S. Landranger 143/Explorer 236
Grid reference 598113

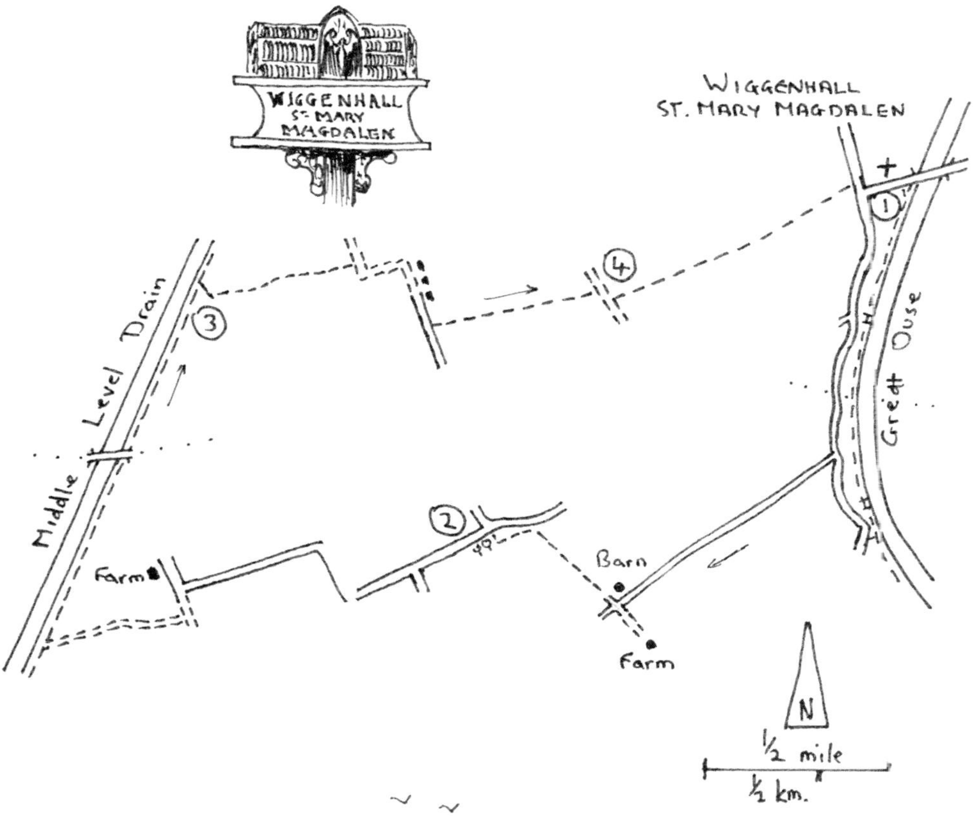

Marshland is that part of the Fens, mainly the northern area, consisting of the rich silt lands won from the sea. To the south, and inland, lie the black peat Fens reclaimed from the drained bogs and marshes.

Both produce some of the finest, and most fertile, soils in the country.

Here is a marshland walk that, ideally needs a bright, dry and sunny day to enjoy comfortably. Any sign of dampness and stout boots and waterproof trousers are strongly recommended. It is definitely not a bare leg walk, for it is amazing how much water standing crops and lush grass can hold. With one notable exception, little has been done to ease the passage of walkers, although several paths have been well signposted.

St. Mary Magdalen, one of four Wiggenhalls (St. Germans, St. Peters, St. Mary the Virgin and St. Mary Magdalen) stands to the south of St. Germans, about six miles from Lynn.

1. - From the church walk towards the fairly new bridge spanning the Great Ouse, and turn right along the riverbank opposite The Cock Inn. Follow this easy riverbank path south and through a kissing gate. The path may be rather lush past the abutments of the old rail bridge (the Magdalen Road to Wisbech branch) until the next pair of kissing gates is reached.

100 yards past them turn right down off the bank through a gate onto the road, by the 30 mph speed limit signs. Turn right along the road to the junction on your left, and turn along this 'No Through Road'. Follow for about half a mile to turn right along a signposted grassy track - just past a brick barn and opposite a farm road. This track becomes rather overgrown and it may be necessary for you to follow the field-edge alongside.

As you progress you pass a narrow ditch on your right and just before the road the path swings left alongside a wide and deep ditch to a low, grassy culvert spanning it, opposite a small plantation. Cross this 'bridge' to the road.

2. - Turn left along the road and through a sharp right, then left bend to farm buildings on another sharp right bend. This section gives an unrivalled 360 degree panorama and opportunity to try identifying landmarks on the distant horizon.

At this junction turn left past the trees and then right along a grassy bridleway. This leads to the Middle Level Drain, which was constructed to carry water directly from the drained lands by the Cambridgeshire border to the Great Ouse at Wiggenhall St. Germans.

Here turn right along the bank path (again, if rather overgrown, it may be necessary to follow the field-edge). Cross the old railway and continue for just under $^1/_2$ mile to where a meandering drain goes off to the right.

3. - Turn right and cross the narrow field along an unmarked path to the plank bridge across a drain. Cross and pick up the narrow field-edge path with the drain on your right. This leads to a track. Bear right and it soon becomes a tarmac lane past houses. About 100 yards past the houses (and by an electricity pole) turn left along a signposted path across the field to a hedge end. Now follow the field-edge path ahead to where a grassy track crosses.

4. - Turn right and almost immediately left along another path with a ditch and hedge on your right. This path improves as you progress towards the distant tower of St. Mary Magdalen.

At the road turn right and then left, along Church Road back into the centre of the village and the 15th. century church.

7 - Castle Acre & West Acre

Distance: 6 mls - 9.7 km (about 2.5 hours)

O.S. Landranger 132/Explorer 236
Grid reference 817151

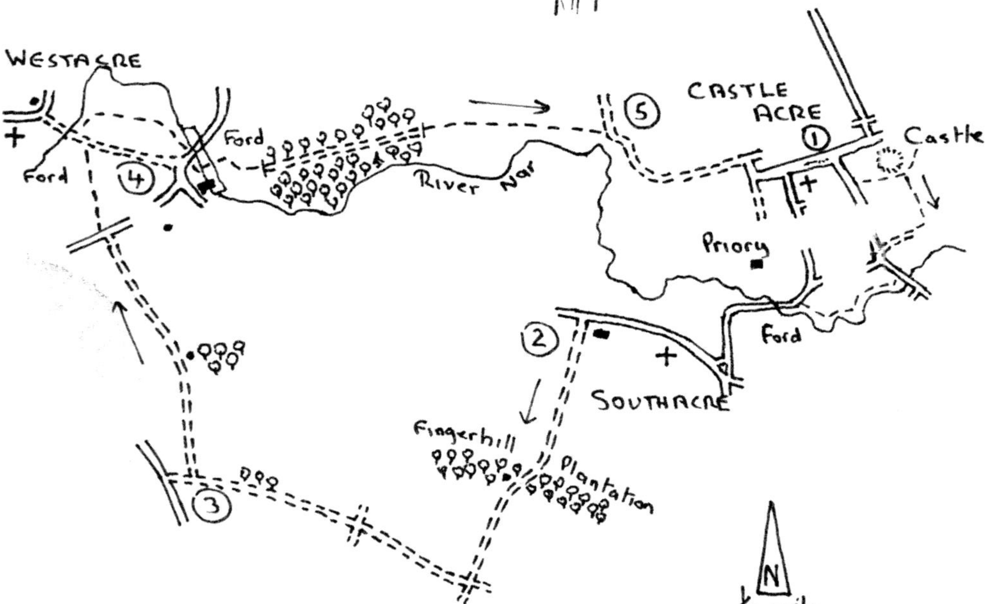

This walk explores the three 'Acres' Castle Acre (once East Acre), Southacre, and Westacre. They stand along a charming and peaceful stretch of the Nar valley - Norfolk's 'Holy Land'. The main settlement, Castle Acre, stands at the crossing point where several ancient trackways, the most notable being Peddars Way, cross this river.

1. - Start from Stocks Green, in the heart of the village, and turn right through the massive Bailey Gate into Bailey Street - now part of Peddars Way. Just past the Old Red Lion turn left along a path to the castle. There a modern wooden bridge gives access to the Upper Ward and there are good views from the top of these earthworks. Turn right and head straight down the massive Lower Ward to a narrow path by the left edge of the old wall. Drop down to a path running along by the bungalow and turn right into a short lane (Cuckstool Lane) to the lower end of Bailey Street. Bear left along the road, passing Blind Lane junction on your right to a gap in the hedge, just before the river bridge. Here a stile leads along a good, raised path through the water meadow. This excellent, winding path is a permissive path, but welcome for all that for it is a fine stretch. The path joins a lane (Southacre Road) and you bear left to the ford. Here pause awhile to soak up the atmosphere of this view across to William de Warenne's fine 11th. century Cluniac Priory. Continue along the lane and at a junction take the right fork, leading through the tiny hamlet of Southacre, almost hidden in the trees. Pass the modest church of St. George, gently resting after the exertions of alteration and rebuilding during its first centuries, to follow past a large mellow farm and hall.

2. - Immediately past them turn left along a hedged, sandy track that eventually passes through a narrow belt of trees - Fingerhill Plantation - and a small cottage. Continue to the 'crosstracks' and turn right alongside the hedge. Cross another track and pass a triangular clump of trees, then along a more open field edge to where (about 100 yards before a road) a waymarked track goes off to the right.

3. - Turn right downhill and past some farm buildings to the road, with views across to West Acre church. Cross the road and follow the path opposite along the field edge. At the narrow, hedged track turn left for a few yards before turning right by some pine trees, onto the gorse-covered heath.

(As a short, pleasant addition, the lane continues over a nearby ford into West Acre offering more Priory ruins, a church with an unusual clock-face and, perhaps, a welcome pub).

Back at the common, follow the path across the heath to a lane and ford opposite Mill House.

(A short distance away, on the far side of the Southacre Road, and almost hidden in a thicket of trees, stand the low broken fragments of St. Bartholomew's Chapel, Custhorpe).

4. - At the ford turn right, uphill for 50 yards and left through a squeeze. This path leads over two good, footbridges and across the water-meadow, and gives a good view of the watermill. Cross the meadow slightly rightward to a gate and stile onto a track (Mill Lane) that leads alongside the wood before emerging onto the old water-meadows with the River Nar flowing quietly by on the right. Follow this to a kissing-gate onto a lane.

5.- Turn right and follow the lane as it gently curves uphill to a junction. Turn right for a few yards before turning left (just before the Priory gateway and entrance) past the church to the delights offered on all sides at Stocks Green.

8 – Bawsey & Roydon Common

Distance: 7.5 mls - 12.1 km (about 3 hours)

O.S. Landranger 132/Explorer 23 (250)
Grid reference 675198

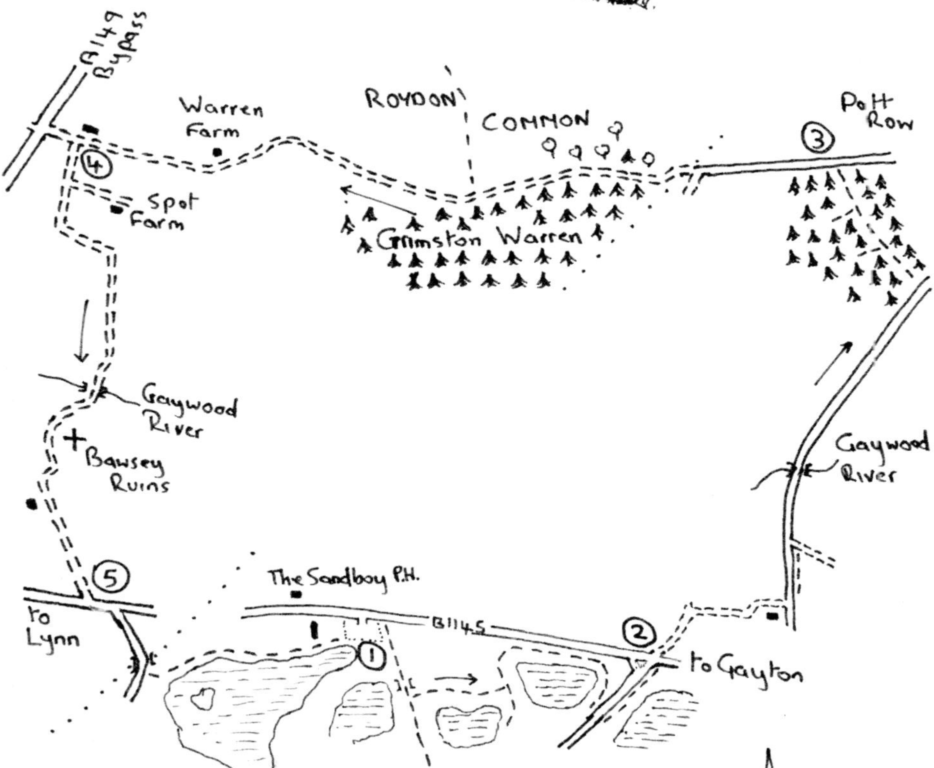

That "Rising was a seaport town, when Lynn was but a marsh...." was graphically illustrated on the TV archaeology programme Time Team when the map of West Norfolk was redrawn showing the ancient coastline. As most of Lynn was flooded with blue, leaving just the original manor of Gaywood, part of the Woottons and Castle Rising above the tide, so another slim peninsular stood above the waters, graced by what we know locally as 'Bawsey ruins'. It was shown to have been a settlement far older than the present Norman church of St. James. Indeed a settlement that seems to stretch back to the Neolithic period.

1. - Start from the Leziate Country Park main car-park, near the Sandboy public house in Bawsey, on the B1145 Gayton Road. With your back to the road bear left across the parking area and grass to a power-line that runs almost due south along the edge of the car-park. Here a grassy path (one of the original rights of way) follows this line gently uphill for 300 yards to cross an iron footbridge. Immediately after, turn left and down a wide grassy area, passing a play-area on your left and a sandy beach and lake on your right. Continue ahead uphill to a fence and turn left alongside the RSPB Reserve, almost to the road. Go through the gap and turn right; again along the fence. Follow this rightward to the road. Cross and go through a gap onto another boundary path. Turn left along this, past the sailing lake, to the main road.

2. - Cross the B1145 onto a signposted grass track and follow this for 300 yards to more power-lines. Here your path swings right, along the field-edge, before passing between high hedges and uphill. Cross the open ground leftward and pick up with a track that leads past a bungalow to the road. Turn left along the road for about 20 yards to a gap on your right and follow the signposted field-edge path, parallel with the road, down to a track. Rejoin the road and follow. Cross the young Gaywood River and pass houses. After about 1/2 mile, and just past a phone-box, cross into Pott Row Wood.

In this formerly Forestry Commission land follow the wide ride northward, ignoring any side turnings. This leads out onto a lane (Cliff-en-Howe Road, Pott Row).

3. - Turn left and follow this lane past an assortment of houses. Where a track forks off to the left the lane continues ahead to cross a stream, with white railings, and the former M&GN railway, to pass the much extended, white-clad former crossing-keeper's cottage. Continue along this track past mainly conifer woods of Grimston Warren, and after picking your way gently for a short distance past a spring, the lane becomes more sandy as it rises past Roydon Common toward Warren Farm, and the lane opens out to give distant views of Lynn's skyline. Continue past the farm and enjoy your first views of Bawsey ruins.

4. - By cottages, and a few yards short of the bypass, turn left along a semi-surfaced lane. This becomes sandy after passing the Spot Farm junction. Follow the track over the Gaywood River and up the slope to St. James church, Bawsey, ruined for the last two centuries. From the ruins look across to Lynn; across what was once water, to two tall pylons that mark the present mouth of the Great Ouse, some 3 1/2 miles away. Continue past Church Farm to the main road.

5. - Turn left for 50 yards and then right, along a narrow lane that leads over the old M&GN railbridge. Just over turn sharp left (by the gates) and follow back to the car-park keeping the lake on your right.

9 - Downham Mkt & Wimbotsham

Distance: 8 mls - 12.9 km (about 3.5 hours)

O.S. Landranger 143/Explorer 236
Grid reference 611032

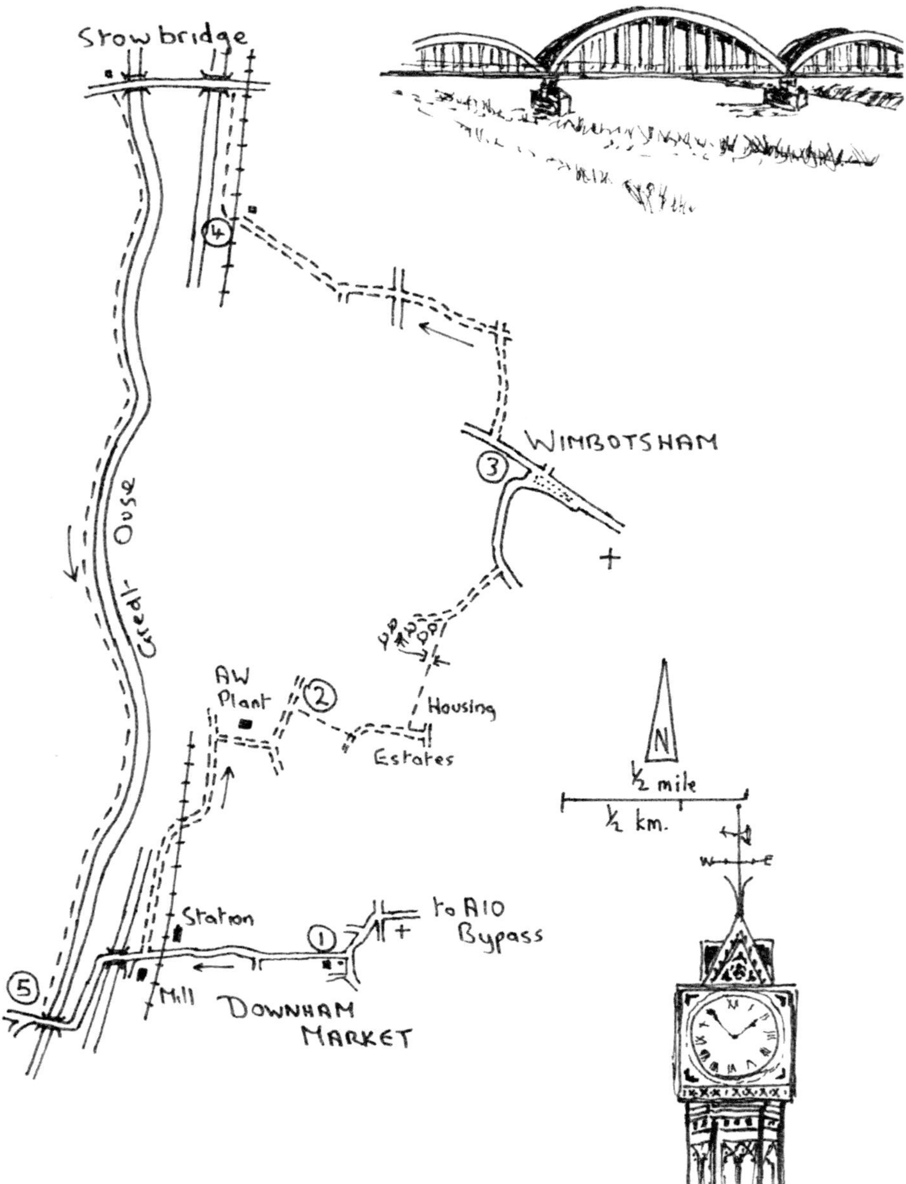

Downham Market is an attractive little town standing on a gentle rise in the Fens about 12 miles south of Lynn. Many of its buildings are made of local carstone, a gingerbread sandstone found more usually on the coast. It still boasts two busy markets - Friday and Saturday - on the small market-place between Cunliffe's Gothic clock tower, presented in 1878 by James Scott, and the Townhall built about ten years later. The butter which once made this market famous is no more.

1. - Starting from the clock tower in the very heart of the town (there is ample free parking in the car-parks around) walk west down Bridge Street, past the Crown Hotel and, after a short distance, a small green to the railway and Heygates Mill. Just over the rail-line turn right along Fairfield Road. Pass the small trading estate and follow the road to cross the railway again. Bear left along the concrete track for nearly 1/4 mile to the Anglian Water treatment works boundary fence. Turn right along a concrete path alongside the fence and at the T-junction turn left again along a narrow track. Keep along the boundary fence and, just after it ends, a small concrete footpath marker on your right indicates a narrow path across the next two fields.

2. - Follow this path and where it joins a track running around the backs of the bungalows bear left around these properties and follow for 200 yards to a path on your left, about 20 yards before an estate road. Turn left along this narrow path, still skirting the edge of houses, to cross a stream before passing a wood. Beyond the wood you join an open track that heads for distant Wimbotsham's rooftops and church to the road. Turn left along the road to Wimbotsham's village green.

This quiet village lies just west of the old Lynn to Downham road, and in 1835 witnessed the landing of a certain Mr Green, 'the Aeronaut', who descended here after a flight in his balloon from London.

On the green, the village sign has an aviation scene from a later age as it depicts one of the bombers stationed nearby during World War II.

3. - Turn left along Westway toward Stow Bridge. After 250 yards turn right along a signposted track - Honey Hill. Follow past the houses and continue to a 'crossroads' of tracks. Turn left along a broad green lane or loke and, just after passing a large pond on your right, cross a road. Continue ahead along the track, past the woods and continue to the rail crossing.

4. - Cross the line, climb the bank and turn right along the Relief Channel - built as a result of the 1953 flood disaster to take additional fenland waters from Denver to Lynn thereby relieving the Great Ouse. Continue to the bridge. Turn left over the Relief Channel bridge and then over the brand new, just opened Stow Bridge (formerly a smaller version of Lynn's old 'Cut Bridge'). Opposite the East Anglian Field Study Centre - once The Crown - turn left along the west bank of the tidal Great Ouse and head south back toward Downham Market. The Great Ouse remains tidal to Denver Sluice, a couple of miles south of Downham and, as the Hundredfoot or New Bedford River, as far as Earith. Now follows a splendid stretch of riverbank with wide views across the rich 'silt marshland' fields. The black peat fenlands lie more to the south of the town. Follow the riverbank to the road.

5. - Turn left over the bridge and follow the roadside pavement back toward Downham. Recross the Relief Channel and, repassing Heygates Mill, follow Bridge Street back into the town centre.

10 – Hunstanton & Ringstead

Distance: 8 mls - 12.9 km (about 3.5 hours) *O.S. Landranger 132/Explorer 23 (250)*
Grid reference 676420

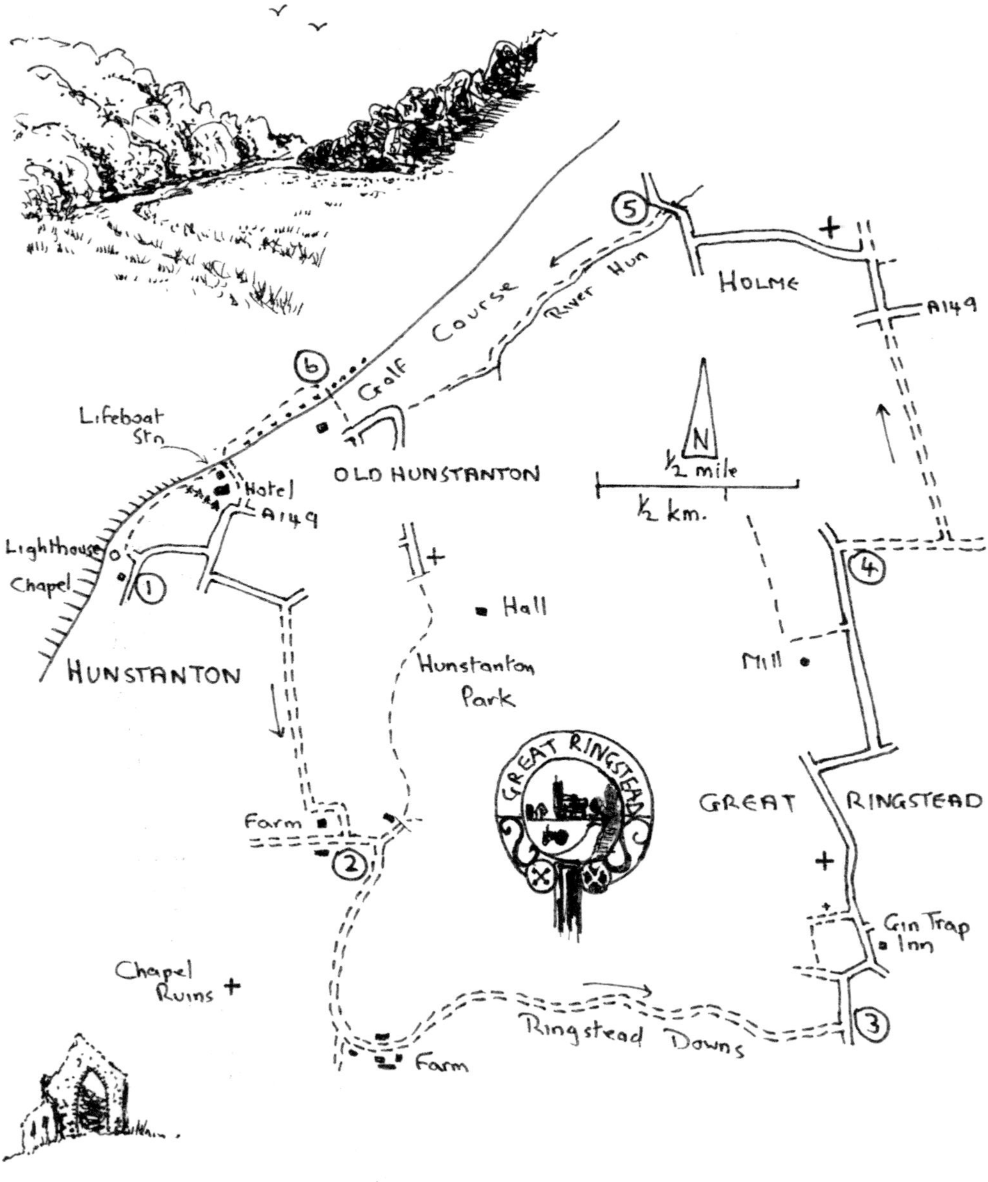

The north-west corner of Norfolk has been dominated and shaped for many centuries by the manor of le Strange. The connection goes back over 800 years to when the estate was inherited from its Domesday owners. Deemed hereditary Lord High Admiral of the Wash, the head of the family claimed possession of anything either on the beach or in the sea as far as a man can ride a horse and throw a spear.

The remains of the family home, Hunstanton Hall, once a moated mansion, stand secluded in a thickly wooded park.

1. - Start from near the clifftop remains of St. Edmund's Chapel, founded by the martyr saint as a thanks-offering following his shipwreck here on his way to be crowned King of the Angles.

There is some parking along Cliff Parade or the nearby pay car-park. From the end of Lighthouse Close bear left along Lighthouse Lane to the main coast road. Turn right for 100 yards to turn left along Chapel Bank Lane. On a left bend turn sharp right along a hedged, green lane. Follow south with views across to the wooded Hunstanton Park, and to the old water-tower atop Redgate Hill. The lane bends down to a junction (Downs Road).

2. - Turn left along to a sharp right turn. (The track ahead crosses Hunstanton Hall Park to Old Hunstanton church, but is only open to the public on THURSDAYS). Turn right to follow the avenue of mature oak and sycamore and after passing the nearby ruins of St. Andrew's chapel, bear left past the farm buildings of Downs Farm - including a fine old pantiled cart-shed and hayloft. This was Barrett Ringstead or Ringstead Parva and stands on the springline.

Go through the fieldgate onto Ringstead Downs. The track winds through this magnificent dry chalk valley, past a wealth of wild flowers and plants. Continue to the Ringstead road.

3. - Turn left toward Great Ringstead. On the sharp bend by the duck pond turn left along Hall Lane (a right turn leads through the village past the Gin Trap Inn). From the pond Hall Lane passes several bungalows; and the remains of St. Peter's church stand by Hall Farm.

By the speed limit sign turn right along a grassy path which leads past cottages to Chapel Lane. Turn right to the main road and left onto the modern Peddars Way. Pass the village store, and the remaining church of St. Andrew's.

All but the tower of St. Peter's was pulled down in 1771 to repair Great Ringstead's (Ringstead Magna) and the parishes consolidated.

Continue to the road junction and turn right into Holme Road and left into Peddars Way North. Follow past the former 6-sailed tower mill. Just beyond Peddars Way turns off for its final descent to the sea, but follow the road for a further 150 yards.

4. - Turn right along an open track (Green Bank). Views across the Wash show the Lincolnshire coast from Boston Stump to Skegness. After 400 yards turn left down a 'holloway' to the coast road. Cross into Northgate Road and follow through Holme-next-the-Sea and past St. Mary's church. At the T-junction, opposite a pond, turn right to rejoin Peddars Way to a bridge.

5. - Cross the River Hun and immediately turn left onto the Coast Path alongside to Hunstanton. The path skirts the golf course to a road. Bear right along the road for 100 yards to a gap (opposite the end of a lane) and turn right across the golf-course - take care. Pass chalets to the beach and turn left.

6. - Follow the beach to the Lifeboat Station and cafe and turn right by the front of the Lifeboat Station to follow the sandy, waymarked Coast Path to the gently climbing cliffs, lighthouse and chapel.

11 - Snettisham & The Wash Coast

Distance: 8 mls - 12.9 km (about 3.5 hours)

O.S. Landranger 132/Explorer 23 (250)
Grid reference 648335

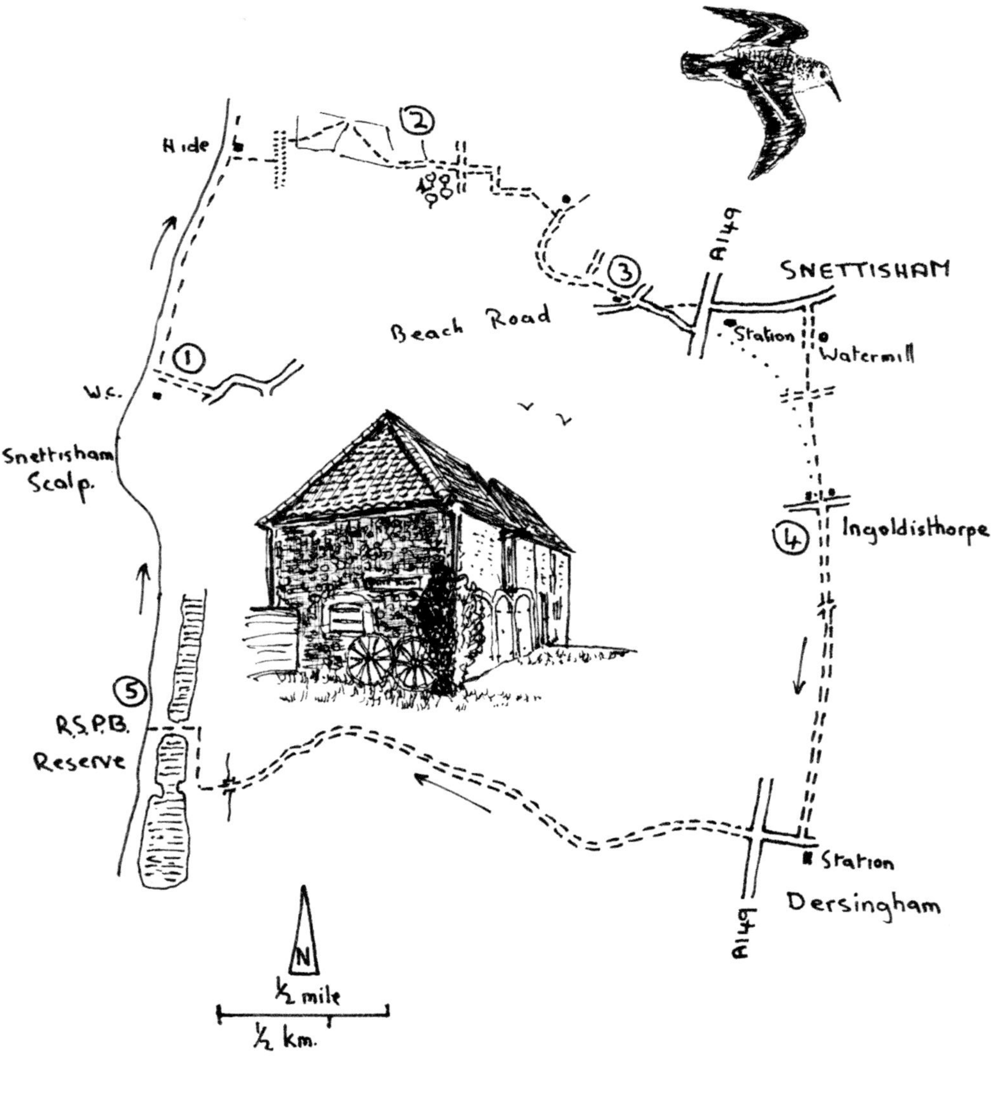

When the great Beeching axe fell across so many of our rural railways over 30 years ago, and the lines were chopped up, destroyed or built over, many - not just enthusiasts - said rural railways would be needed again. We are now seeing that resurgence in increasing rail traffic and even re-opened lines. Many lines were rescued as heritage lines, but now old routes are being re-examined for full commercial services. Fortunately many of the old lines that did not become bypasses or built upon were retained as paths, cycleways and bridleways.

Whether the Lynn to Hunstanton line can ever be re-opened is very doubtful; however, sections can still be walked and cycled, and a well-used footpath exists along part of this coastal walk.

1. - Start from the pay car-park at the beach end of Beach Road, Snettisham. For free parking use the parking area by the Common (Point 3). Walk northwards along the beach shingle bank. There are great views all round - ahead to the town and cliffs of Hunstanton, west across The Wash to Boston Stump and the Lincolnshire coast to Skegness, south to the towers of Lynn, and east across to the wooded hills of Lodge Hill and Ken Hill.

After about $^{3}/_{4}$ mile you come to a wooden hide. Here turn right and follow a narrow path (with coloured marker-posts) across the rough ground to the inner seabank. Climb and turn left for a few yards before turning right down to a grassy 'bridge' over the river (by the Country Park sign) to a fieldgate and kissing-gate onto the marsh pasture. This path leads from the beach over Lodge Hill into Snettisham and was used by local fishermen to gain access to their boats at Three Banks End.

Follow the path diagonally left to a gap in the far corner and turn **sharp** right, through another gateway, and bear left across the next pasture, then through another gap to continue parallel with the right-hand hedge to a field gate.

2. - Go through and keep ahead along a wood-side track. Cross over the old rail-line and follow the hedged track ahead. This turns sharp right and then left towards the farm. It then forks to the right of a former barn, along a new hedge, before turning right along a hedged path that runs around Lodge Hill. Follow this path around the foot of the hill and through a gate before bearing right down a narrower path to the Common and former rail gatehouse to Beach Road.

3. - At the road bear left, passing Common Road, and keep ahead. On a slight right bend leave the road to the cars and follow the old 'dead' section to the bypass and cross into Station Road. Pass the station buildings and continue into Snettisham. Shortly after passing Ingolside and the Sheepbridge Mobile Home Park you pass a row of six terraced cottages with fine Dutch gables. Just beyond turn right along a signed track past the old Watermill. Cross the Ingol and follow the open path across the field. Cross a track (Coaly Lane) and continue ahead along a faint field-path - with the former rail-line curving in from the right. The field narrows to a funnel and the path crosses a metal-stile between property and the rail-line to a lane (The Drift).

4. - Cross over and follow the railway path ahead. This leads into Dersingham and by the former station turn right along a lane. This crosses the bypass and you follow the concrete road across the fields to the inner seabank. Cross over and turn right along a path beside the RSPB Reserve. This soon turns left over the lagoons to the outer bank and beach.

5. - Turn right and follow the beach, past Snettisham Scalp, and the Sailing club, back to the Shepherd's Port car-park.

12 - Great Massingham

Distance: 8.25 mls - 13.3 km (about 3.5 hours) *O.S. Landranger 132/Explorer 23 (250)*
Grid reference 798229

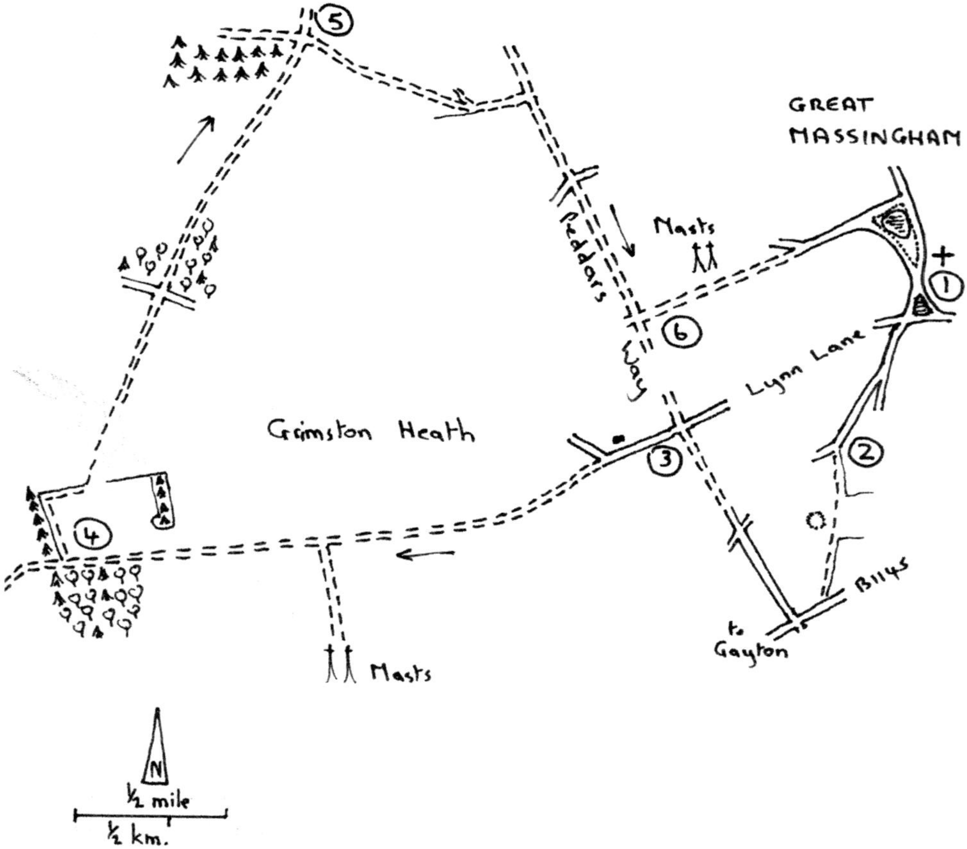

East Anglia - comprising as it does the counties of Norfolk and Suffolk, and the borders of Cambridgeshire and Essex - has always been an isolated area of England.

Bounded by the sea to the north and east, the Fens to the west, and the dense forests of Essex to the south, the only easily accessible link with the rest of England was the chalk ridge that stretches from beyond the Chilterns to the sea at Holme. Along this runs the Icknield Way, and to the east of it the later, Romanised section - Peddars Way.

This chalk contains many rich seams of flint which provided man with his earliest manufacture and trade in tools and weapons. The most extensive of the flint mines that sourced this vital material was probably Grimes Graves, near Brandon in Suffolk; but among other sites in East Anglia was an important group at Great Massingham.

Standing in an area of rich farmland and former heath, the village has had a long and varied history. It has lost its mediaeval market and fair, and the priory (founded in 1260 as a cell to Castle Acre) is gone, its site now occupied by Abbey Farm. Gone too is its second church, All Saints' - but it retains the fine 15th. century church of St. Mary's, along with several ponds.

One of these, Scotsman's Pit, is one of the largest village ponds in England, and of Great Massingham it has been said: "There is as much water as green and a good deal of both".

1. - Start from near the splendid church (please avoid parking on the grass) and walk south along the Castle Acre road, passing the village well, the sign, and the junction with Lynn Lane, opposite a pond on your left. After a further 300 yards, fork right along Drunken Drove and after about a $^{1}/_{4}$ mile - on a right bend - a gap on the left leads into a field.

2. - Now keep ahead along the signposted bridleway with a hedge on your left. Follow this over the rise and where the hedge breaks away to the left keep ahead past a tree-filled hollow on your right. Pick up with the hedge again and continue down, through a second field, to the road.

Turn right for a few yards to Peddars Way and turn right to follow this ancient trackway. Cross a road, and continue to the next junction (Lynn Lane).

3. - Turn left along the road past Heath Cottages and, on the sharp right bend, fork left along a sandy track across Grimston Heath for nearly two miles, passing a track to two radio masts on your left. Continue past the wood, and then a small conifer belt (complete with neat surrounding hedge), both on your right. Pass a wood on your left to the next tree belt that crosses the track.

4. - Here turn right and follow the signposted field-edge path. Then turn to follow the fence rightward for about 200 yards to a gap. Turn left along the left field-edge to where it becomes a hedged track and continue to the road and cross. Continue for over a mile to where, after passing a track and small clump of trees on your left, a long belt of trees comes in from the left to join the track and there is a 'crossroads'.

5. - Turn right along a hedged lane, then a left field-edge. A path joins from the left and after a few yards the lane joins Peddars Way. Turn right and walk southward along this fine and wide lane. Cross the Little Massingham road and continue to a left junction.

6. - Turn left along this track - Greengate Lane, past more radio masts, and continue to the road - Walcups Lane. Follow this past houses back to the village centre. Bear right, passing the large pond back to the church and the green.

13 - The Creakes

Distance: 8.5 mls - 13.7 km (about 3.5 hours)

O.S. Landranger 132/Explorer 24 (251)
Grid reference 856362

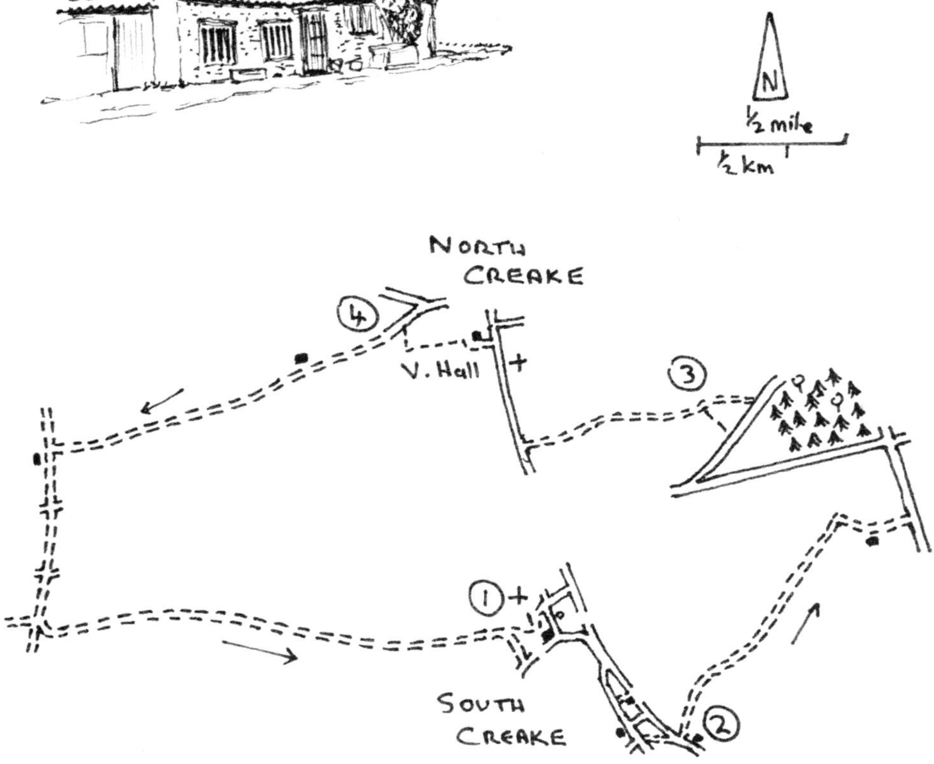

North and South Creake stand linked by the silver thread of the tiny River Burn as it heads northwards to the coast. This walk follows the gentle, well-hedged lanes that flow from this shallow valley and passes two fine, mediaeval churches.

1. - Start from the fine church of Our Lady St. Mary - described by the late Sir John Betjeman as "One of those perfect village churches. It glows with light and whiteness, and I think it almost the most beautifully furnished and alive church I have seen in East Anglia".

Walk south between the neat fruit-trees of Bluestone Farm (so named after a blue boulder - a glacial erratic - found here) and the tree-fringed pond opposite.

Passing the great brick barn turn left at the junction (Bluestone Road) over the clear waters of the Burn to the main road by the Primary School Cottage. Bear right and recross the river into Back Street. This leads to The Green, but about midway along look out for the tall tower on your left; this was the former brewery that became the Ace Blade Works (safety razor blade manufacturers).

From the store and Post Office cross The Green to the village sign and bridged ford. The sign depicts, on one side the bloody battle that took place a thousand years ago amid local earthworks when defending Saxons fought the invading Danes. The road leading to that site is still known as Bloodgate Hill. A more tranquil St. Mary's is depicted on the reverse. Note too the packet of Farmers Glory, the first British cereal it was claimed, and produced at the highly mechanised and innovative Bluestone Farm. Bear right along the main road to The Ostrich.

2. - Cross and take the track that climbs up out of the valley. Eventually this green lane or 'loke' is joined by a stony track to swing past Whin Close Villa to the road. Turn left to the crossroads and then left again past the dark firs of East Common. At the next junction turn sharp right towards the distant Holkham woods. After $^1/_4$ mile and by a hedge on your left (by a power-line) turn left alongside the hedge, keeping it to your left.

3. - At the track turn left, along the parish boundary between the two Creakes, to eventually drop down to the main road. Turn right into North Creake. Take care, there is no pavement.

A short distance beyond St. Mary's church turn left by the village hall. (For those in search of refreshments the tea-rooms are a few yards further along the road, and The Jolly Farmers about 200 yards beyond).

The gravel path passes over the Burn once again and behind the village hall you pick up with the signposted field-path. This open path leads up to, and then along a hedge, to continue as an open grassy path before swinging right down to a lane.

4. - Turn left along this lane to the farm. Immediately past the farm keep ahead for about a mile along a wide grass field-edge to a tarmac lane. This old lane runs south from Burnham Market (about 2 miles north) to Syderstone (about 2 miles south).

Turn left and head south. Pass over two 'crossroads' and at the third turn left again. This is literally one of the high points of the walk - at some 223ft (68m). This track now heads eastward to eventually drop back down into the Burn Valley once more, and South Creake. Finally where the lane swings sharply away to the right keep ahead along a narrow, signposted, and fenced path with the hedge on your left. This leads out by cottages back to the church.

14 - Docking & Bircham

Distance: 8.75 mls - 14.1 km (about 4 hours)

O.S. Landranger 132/Explorer 23 (250)
Grid reference 766370

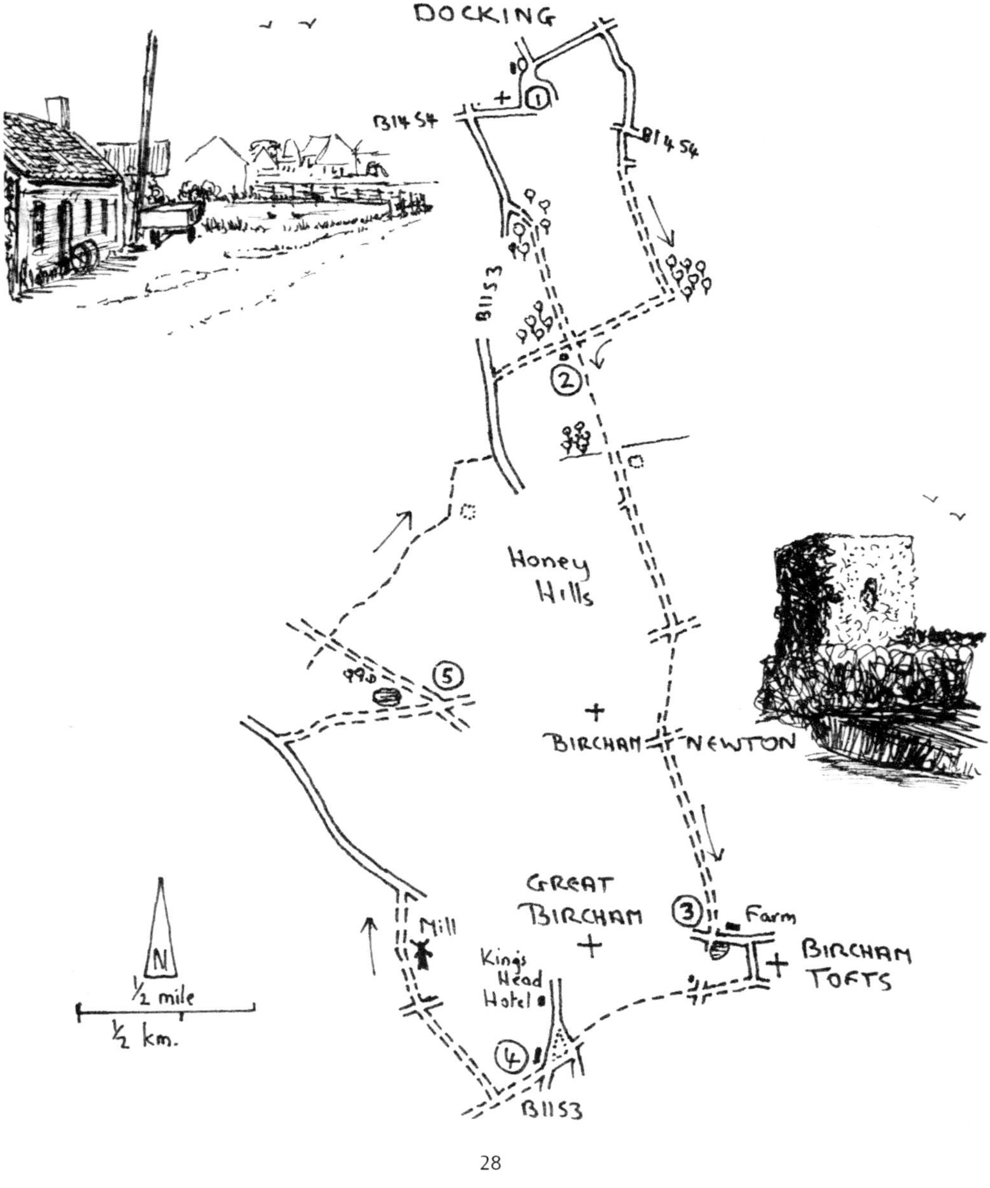

At 290 ft above sea-level (the metric 88m. doesn't sound as impressive), "Dry Docking" is the highest point in West Norfolk. Standing well above the chalk streams and springline this small township has had to rely on wells for its water supply.

In 1760, Catherine Henley (one of the local Hare family) was responsible for the sinking of the Town Well over 200 ft. deep. An inscription on the modern plaque on the site recalls the original: "O Ye Wells Bless Ye the Lord, With Thee is the Well of Life".

On this site, in Well Street, in 1928 a large water-tower was erected which dominated the scene for many years until pulled down and replaced by a reservoir and tower on the outskirts.

1. - Start from the 14th. century church of St. Mary's Docking - there is some parking along the wide road between the church and school. Walk northward past the forge and pond and turn right along Pound Lane. Nearby stood the old Town-Well and later water-tower. Follow to the crossroads and turn right, along Bradmere Lane. From this high point are views across to the Burnhams and Station Road, part of the village behind. Cross High Street into Mill Lane and where the tarmac ends keep ahead along the track. By a small wood this turns right to a junction by a wood, and the remains of an old stone barn.

2. - Here turn sharp left, past the ruins and, skirting the soil heap, follow a narrow field-path south; aim just to the left of a small wood. Go through the rather fragmented hedge to pick up with a clear track ahead with a hedge on your right, and past a small pit on your left.

This track becomes open and then has another hedge on your right. Passing a raised water-tank, cross a track, and keep ahead along a field-edge path, with the hedge now on your left. Along here may be seen the hangars of the former Bircham Newton Airfield, together with the tower-cranes of the Construction Industry College. Ahead lies Great Bircham, and rightward may be seen the popular Bircham Mill. To your right is the simple church of Bircham Newton. Here lived Horatia, daughter of those famous lovers, Admiral Lord Horatio Nelson, and Lady Hamilton; for Horatia married Philip Ward, Rector of Bircham Newton. Cross another track and follow the hedged lane down into Bircham.

3. - At the road by the farm, and opposite the pond, turn left for 200 yards before turning right down the lane past the crumbling, ivy-covered remains of St. Andrews, Bircham Tofts. Rather sad and neglected it stands mouldering amid an overgrown graveyard of tottering headstones. At the junction turn right along a green lane. Cross another, by a cottage, and follow the track ahead with its view across the fields to St. Mary's, to a small green and village sign, near the King's Head Hotel.

4. - Cross the main road to a lane just left of the large, stone and brick barn, now converted into a home. Follow this lane about 200 yards to a junction before turning right along a hedged lane to a road. Cross and keep ahead to the fine tower-mill (1846) and tearoom.

Follow the tarmac lane past the mill to the next junction and turn left. Follow this country lane for almost $^1/_2$ mile to where a green lane turns sharply right. Turn right and follow this, with a clear little stream bubbling alongside, past a large pond and across a shallow ford.

5. - At the cross-tracks turn sharp left and climb gently past a small wood to a hedge crossing. Turn right along the field-edge path and follow for $^3/_4$ mile to the road. Cross and turn left for $^1/_4$ mile to a track on your right. Turn right alongside the hedge to the wood and barn ruins (Point 2). Here turn left past the woods to the road again. Bear right along this to the crossroads. Turn right past the Pound, cottages and pond to the churchyard. A path around the church leads back to the start.

15 – Barton Bendish & Beachamwell

Distance: 10 mls - 16.1 km (about 4.5 hours)

O.S. Landranger 143/Explorer 236
Grid reference 712056

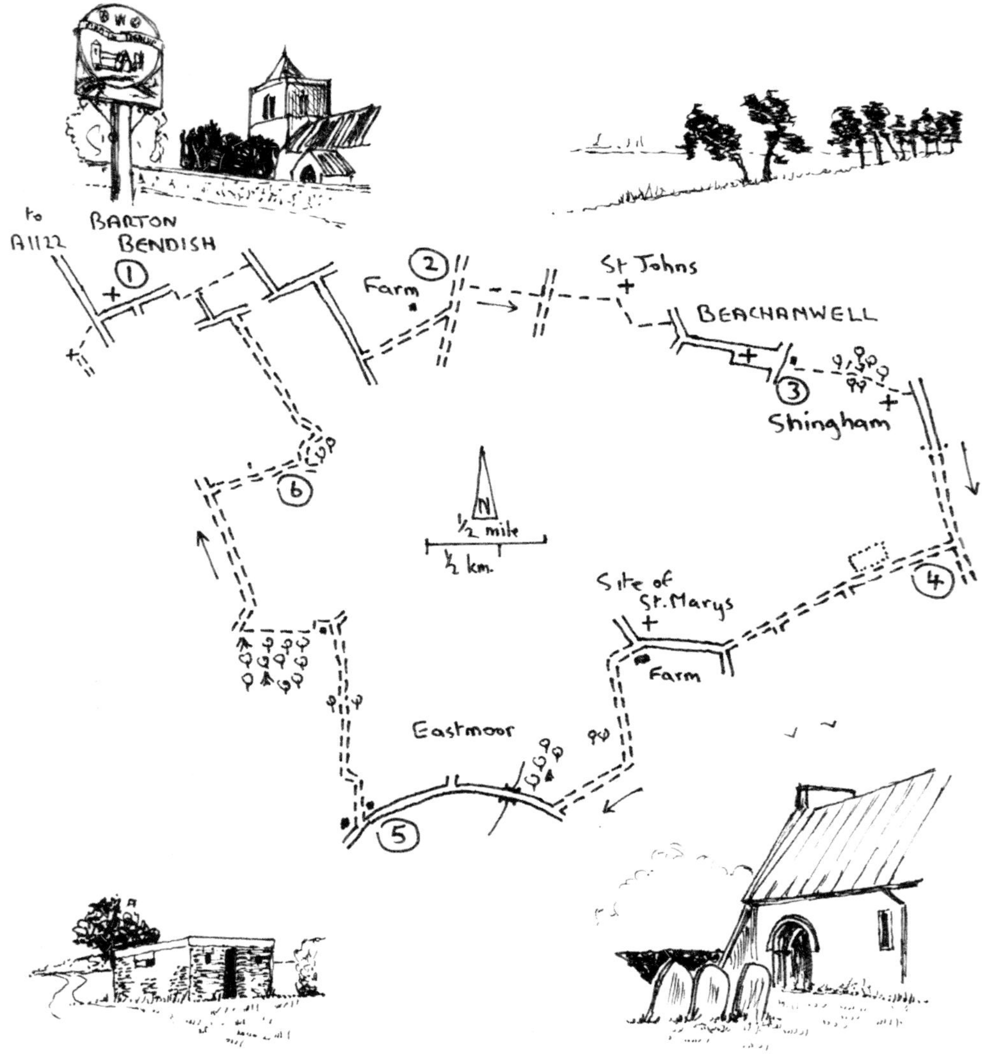

Barton Bendish and Beachamwell lie along the northern side of the Wissey valley. It is a rich and fertile landscape with a strong springline giving good feeder-streams into the main River Wissey. It is a varied landscape. This route passes active, redundant, ruined or the sites of, seven churches. Both villages boasted at least three churches each. Beachamwell still has St. Mary's; All Saints and St. John's are just ruins. There is said to have been a fourth. Barton Bendish has St. Andrew's, and St. Mary's (Redundant Churches Fund). The third, All Saints, was pulled down to provide material for St. Mary's and a road(!) over two hundred years ago.

1. - Start from the church of St. Andrew's, Barton Bendish, and walk eastward. Just before a stone gateway at the end of the road turn right along a signposted pathway that soon turns left to follow the field-edge. Cross a lane and continue to a second, by white rails and houses. Turn right to the next road junction and turn left along the tree-lined Beachamwell Road. At the next junction turn right along Eastmoor Road. After 600 yards, turn left, by trees, along a farm track. Follow past farm buildings and at the next junction turn left.

2. - At the next field boundary turn right and follow the path alongside the hedge to Green Drove. Cross, slightly rightward, to a robust stile. Cross and continue ahead, following the hedge. This eventually leads to another stile by St. John's. Cross and bear rightward to a third stile in the far corner. This leads out along a grassy track to two sentinel pines at the road-edge. At the road turn right and then left into Beachamwell. After passing St. Mary's continue to the far end of the Green where stands The Great Danes Head, or The Great Danes Head (second version) or The Hole in the Wall; and all before a drink (!).

3. - Pass to the right of the pub, and follow the waymarked grassy path ahead. Bear left, through a gap, to the electricity pole, and then right to continue eastward along the field-edge path (hedge on your right). This soon enters a wood. Follow ahead and ignore any side turnings. At the far end cross a railed footbridge and bear right across grass to the road, by the left end of conifers around Shingham church. Turn right along the road. St. Botolph's is a small, ancient church sans tower but with a fine Early Norman doorway. Continue along the road which, once past Shingham Farm, becomes a track. Follow this for a further $^{1}/_{2}$ mile to a right junction.

4. - Turn right along this track (along the line of electricity poles). Follow westward for about a mile to the road - passing a large embanked water reservoir on your right. At the road continue ahead passing Caldecote Farm. Where the road then bears right (the mound on your right marks the site of St. Mary's church, Oxborough) bear left along a track that goes around the back of the farm before passing through woods to the Eastmoor road. Turn right along the road and cross a small stream that leads to the Wissey. Pass the road junction in Eastmoor, and continue ahead (signed Stoke Ferry) over a low hill and past a 'clunch' cottage, and modern bungalows opposite. Continue gently downhill to another cottage.

5. - Turn right and follow the signposted trackway northward for over $^{1}/_{2}$ mile to a barn. Swing left past this and through the hedge. Bear left around the field-edge and alongside the wood. Follow this rough path for 400 yards or so to a waymark and turn right to join a good farm track. This again heads roughly northward and you follow for about $^{1}/_{2}$ mile to a waymarked track (by a large concrete farm-stand). Turn right along this and, after passing the World War II 'pillbox', continue to a small wood.

6. - Turn left and follow this track to the road. Turn left and then right, along Blacksmith's Lane. At the trees turn left and follow the outward route back into the centre of Barton Bendish.

16 - Sandringham

Distance: 12 mls - 19.3 km (about 5.5 hours) *O.S. Landranger 132/Explorer 23 (250)*
Grid reference 690288

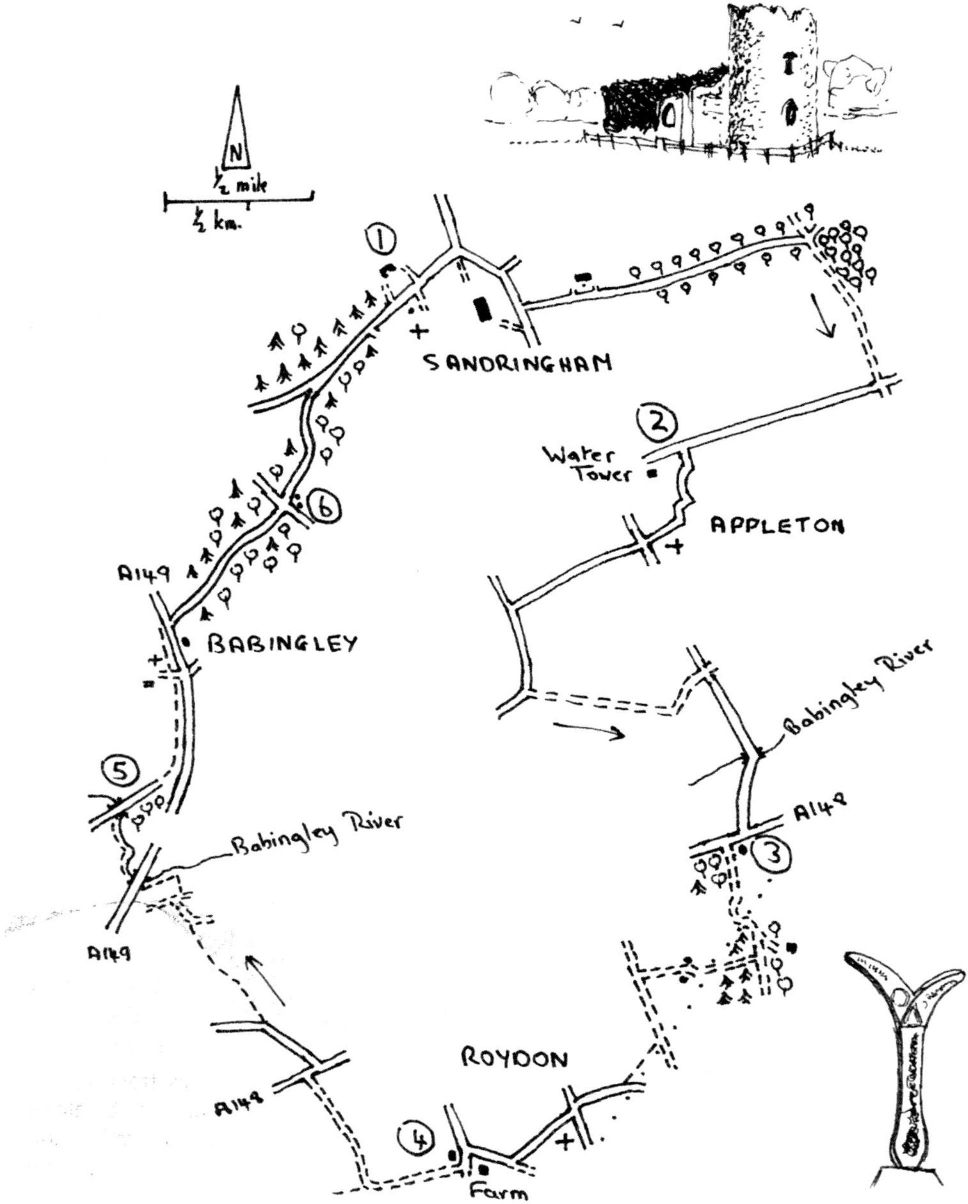